MARSHALL MINI

BUGS

A Marshall Edition
Conceived, edited and designed by
Marshall Editions Ltd
The Orangery
161 New Bond Street
London W1Y 9PA

First published in the UK in 2000 by
Marshall Publishing Ltd

10 9 8 7 6 5 4 3 2 1

ISBN 1 84028 356 4

Originated in Singapore by HBM
Printed in China by Imago

Consultant: Dr Bryan Turner
Senior Designer: Edward Simkins
Design Manager: Ralph Pitchford
Art Director: Simon Webb
Managing Editor: Kate Phelps
Editorial Director: Cynthia O'Brien
Proofreader: Patience Coster
Production: James Bann
Picture Researcher: Antonella Mauro

MARSHALL MINI
BUGS

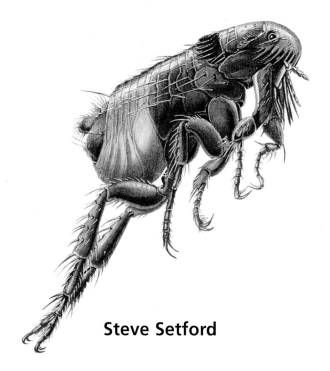

Steve Setford

MARSHALL PUBLISHING • LONDON

Contents

Worker honey bees tend the honeycomb cells in the nest.

The world of bugs

Monarch butterflies feeding.
This species is native to North and
South America.

What are bugs?

The word bug conjures up pictures of small, creeping, crawling creatures. In this book, the term bug refers specifically to insects and spiders, which belong to the arthropod group of animals.

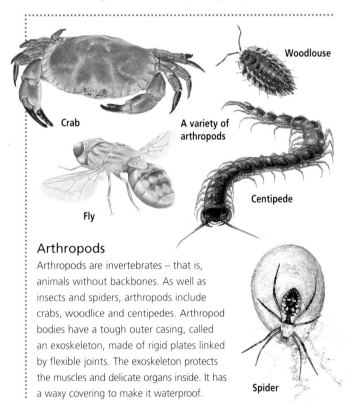

Woodlouse

Crab

A variety of arthropods

Centipede

Fly

Spider

Arthropods

Arthropods are invertebrates – that is, animals without backbones. As well as insects and spiders, arthropods include crabs, woodlice and centipedes. Arthropod bodies have a tough outer casing, called an exoskeleton, made of rigid plates linked by flexible joints. The exoskeleton protects the muscles and delicate organs inside. It has a waxy covering to make it waterproof.

Prehistoric bugs

The first bugs appeared over 300 million years ago. They were the first animals to fly. Most of these species are now extinct, but fossils show that some were similar to the cockroaches and dragonflies of today. Some insects were fossilised after getting trapped in muddy sediments, which later turned to rock. Others got stuck in resin oozing from tree trunks, which hardened to form amber.

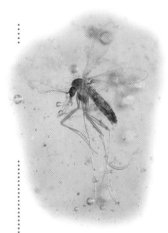

A mosquito fossilised in amber, about 250 million years old.

Other invertebrates

Many non-arthropod invertebrates live in the sea. They include octopus, squid, starfish, sponges, corals and jellyfish. Others, such as snails, slugs and earthworms, live on land. Slugs and snails make a slimy mucus, which helps to stop their bodies drying out and allows them to move more easily. Earthworms spend their lives burrowing through soil.

Snail

Slug

Earthworm

Insects

An arthropod with six legs and a body arranged into three parts – head, thorax and abdomen – is called an insect. There are over a million known species of insects, living in every kind of habitat.

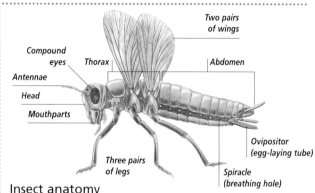

Two pairs of wings

Compound eyes

Thorax

Abdomen

Antennae

Head

Mouthparts

Ovipositor (egg-laying tube)

Three pairs of legs

Spiracle (breathing hole)

Insect anatomy

An insect's thorax has three pairs of legs and, usually, two pairs of wings. (Insects are the only invertebrates that can fly.) The abdomen contains the heart, digestive system and sexual organs. The head carries eyes and antennae, as well as mouthparts, which vary in shape according to the insect's diet. Spongy or tubelike mouthparts mop up or suck up liquid food, while strong jaws chop up prey.

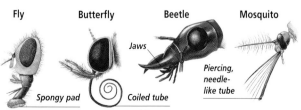

Fly

Butterfly

Beetle

Mosquito

Jaws

Spongy pad

Coiled tube

Piercing, needle-like tube

Moulting

In order to grow to adult size, a young insect must moult – shed its hard exoskeleton – several times during its life. A new skeleton forms beneath the old one, and

A caterpillar wriggles free from its old skin.

when it is ready to moult, the insect splits the old skeleton and wriggles out. Some young insects, such as caterpillars, have soft exoskeletons. They, too, moult several times before they grow a hard exoskeleton as an adult butterfly or moth.

Pollination

To produce seeds, a flower must receive tiny pollen grains from another flower. As insects such as bees and butterflies feed on the pollen and nectar (a sugary liquid) produced by flowers, pollen sticks to their bodies and is spread between flowers.

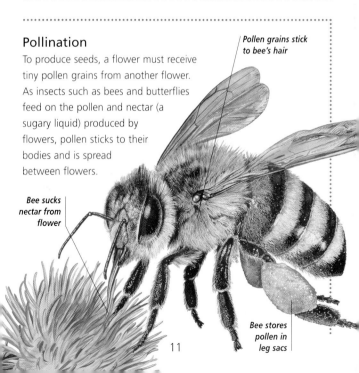

Pollen grains stick to bee's hair

Bee sucks nectar from flower

Bee stores pollen in leg sacs

Arachnids

Arachnids – such as spiders, scorpions and mites – are arthropods that have four pairs of walking legs. There are at least 70,000 different arachnid species, most of which live on land.

Arachnid anatomy

The head and thorax are fused together to form the cephalothorax, which is linked to the abdomen by a narrow waist. At the front of the head are the jaws and mouth. Many arachnids have venom glands that give poisonous bites or stings. The pedipalps are sense organs, which the males also use in mating or for grasping prey.

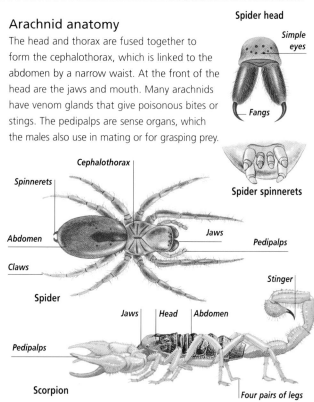

Spider head

Simple eyes

Fangs

Spider spinnerets

Cephalothorax

Spinnerets

Abdomen

Jaws

Pedipalps

Claws

Spider

Stinger

Jaws | *Head* | *Abdomen*

Pedipalps

Scorpion

Four pairs of legs

First few threads anchor the rest of the framework

Web of an orb-weaver

Spokes are added to strengthen the web

Building a web

Some spiders, such as orb-weavers, build silken traps called webs. The silk is produced by glands at the end of the spider's abdomen, emerging from nozzles called spinnerets. Using a type of silk that hardens into a tough thread, the spider weaves a framework that attaches to nearby plants or other supports. It then adds a spiral of a different, sticky silk to trap the prey.

Spider spins a sticky spiral around the web's centre

Waiting on the web

After building its web, a spider waits at the centre or hides close by. A signal thread allows it to detect vibrations caused by struggling prey caught on the web's sticky parts. The spider rushes over, bites the prey and wraps it in silk to stop it escaping. The prey can then be eaten at leisure.

Garden spider with prey wrapped in silken parcel

13

Bug senses

Bugs have antennae and tiny sense hairs that detect smells, tastes, vibrations and sounds. Most bugs have eyes, but sight is less important to them in interpreting the world than it is to us.

Wasp head

A wasp has a pair of large compound eyes that stretch down its cheeks and give it a wide field of view. It also has three simple eyes on the top of its head. The antennae register smells, while tiny sensory hairs detect sounds.

Antennae detect scents in the air

Small, simple eyes detect light and dark

Compound eyes, made up of many tiny lenses, can detect the slightest movement

Talking by touch

Like many bugs, ants communicate with chemical signals. By touching antennae, they can pass on chemical messages.

Two ants communicating.

Avoiding bats

Bats catch insects by sending out high-pitched pulses of sound and detecting the echoes that bounce off prey. Moths have "ears" on their abdomens that can detect these sound-pulses. When a bat swoops in for the kill, a moth escapes by folding up its wings and dropping to the ground.

A bat tries to catch a moth.

Types of antennae

Antennae help an insect discover more about its surroundings. They are sensitive to touch and vibration, and also to airborne scents. Some have many side branches to increase the surface area available for sensory cells and hairs. Arachnids have no antennae, but rely mostly on the sensory hairs on their bodies.

Mosquito's antenna (female)

Cockchafer's antenna

Moth's antenna (male)

Legs and movement

Bugs use their jointed legs to jump, walk, run and much more besides. Crickets, for example, have ears on their knees, and male grasshoppers "sing" to females by rubbing their rear legs against their wings.

Honey bee

Types of legs

Bug legs differ according to their use.

Mole cricket

A cockroach has long, lean legs for running, while a mole cricket uses its broad, muscular legs for digging. Water beetles push through the water with hair-fringed, paddlelike legs, while the hairs on bee legs collect pollen.

Cockroach

Water beetle

Legs for grasping

Many insects have grasping legs, which they use to hold on to the opposite sex when mating, to fight off rivals or to grip prey while feeding. A praying mantis's fore legs have strong muscles; these enable it to clasp struggling prey firmly while it is eating.

Sharp spines grip prey

Praying mantis

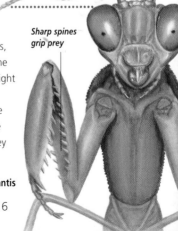

16

Legs for leaping

A cat flea can leap up to 200 times its own length. This remarkable feat is made possible by two rubbery pads at the base of its rear legs. A catch mechanism keeps the pads compressed, like a pair of coiled springs. When the catch is released, the pads expand rapidly, hurling the flea into the air.

Cat flea

Flea uses hooklike claws to hold on to its host's skin

Strong hind legs

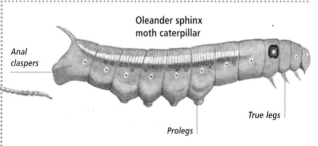

Oleander sphinx moth caterpillar

Anal claspers

True legs

Prolegs

False legs

Like other insects, caterpillars have three pairs of legs on the thorax. They also have five pairs of false legs on the abdomen. These false legs consist of four pairs of muscular projections called prolegs, which have tiny hooks on the end, and a pair of suckerlike anal claspers. Prolegs and claspers help a caterpillar cling on to leaves and stems.

Wings and flight

Arachnids cannot fly, but insects can. Flight enables them to escape from predators and travel far in search of food or a mate. Most insects have two pairs of wings.

The wing cases move forward and spread apart for flight

Large, transparent wings enable a ladybird to achieve surprisingly fast speeds

Ladybird

Wing cases

The fore wings of beetles, such as ladybirds, have evolved into hard, protective wing cases. For flying, beetles only use their hind wings, which are kept folded up beneath the wing cases until it is time for take off.

White-lined sphinx moth

Moth and butterfly wings

The "scaly" fore and hind wings of moths and butterflies are linked so that they flap together. The whirring wings of sphinx moths beat so fast that the moths can hover as they feed on flower nectar.

Aerial stunts

Dragonflies flap their four wings in unison for fast, level flight. But by flapping the fore and hind wings independently, they can perform amazing aerobatics, changing direction rapidly, hovering, stopping in mid-flight and even flying backwards.

The wings are strengthened by a network of veins

Darner dragonfly

Muscles in the thorax pull the wings up and down

Fly halteres

In flies, the hind wings have developed into a pair of clublike structures called halteres. These flap up and down in opposition to the main wings, helping the fly to balance and change direction as it moves through the air. Without them, a fly could not fly.

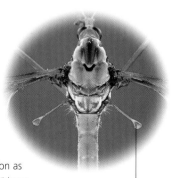

Halteres stick out from the fly's thorax

The life of bugs

Ladybirds gather in large numbers in readiness for hibernation during the cold winter months.

Feeding

Some bugs feed on plants, while others get nourishment by sucking up liquids through strawlike tubes. Many bugs are carnivores (meat eaters), feeding on rotting meat or live prey.

Food liquidisers

Although many flies feed on solid food, they first have to liquefy it. They deposit saliva on the food, which partly dissolves it. They mop up the resulting mushy liquid with a spongy pad on the end of their mouthparts.

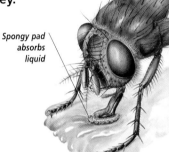

Spongy pad absorbs liquid

Fore legs have taste buds

Nectar drinkers

The feeding tube, or proboscis, of a butterfly or moth coils up under its head. When a moth or butterfly needs to feed, it uncoils the tube, dips it into a flower and sucks up the sugary nectar, just as you would drink through a straw.

Hummingbird sphinx moth

Tube probes deep into flower

Blood suckers

Some bugs feed on blood because it is rich in nutrients. A mosquito pierces an animal's skin with a needlelike tube and then sucks up the blood. It pumps saliva into the wound to stop the blood clotting. Only female mosquitoes bite animals – male mosquitoes feed on nectar.

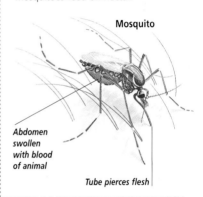

Mosquito

Abdomen swollen with blood of animal

Tube pierces flesh

Blowfly

Leaf chewers

A caterpillar has strong jaws with overlapping teeth to chew up plants. In some caterpillars, the jaws have become flat plates for grinding up leaves. When a caterpillar changes into an adult, its mouthparts turn into a long proboscis.

A caterpillar eating a leaf.

23

Hunters

Many carnivorous bugs are fierce hunters, seeking out victims and killing them with venomous stings or bites, or slicing them up with razor-sharp jaws.

Thread-waisted wasp

A female thread-waisted wasp uses its sting not to kill prey but to paralyse it. She carries it back to her burrow and lays an egg on it. When a grub hatches from the egg, it feeds on the fresh meat of the paralysed prey.

Sting is a modified egg-laying tube, so only females can sting

Thread-waisted wasp with caterpillar prey

Scorpion

A hunting scorpion comes out at night to look for spiders and insects. The scorpion grabs the prey with a pair of large pincers called pedipalps. If the prey is large or struggling, the scorpion uses its sting to paralyse or kill the victim before eating it. The scorpion finds prey mostly by using the fine hairs on its body, which are sensitive to touch.

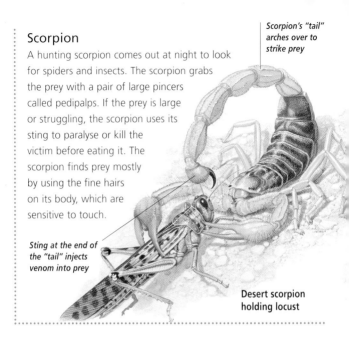

Scorpion's "tail" arches over to strike prey

Sting at the end of the "tail" injects venom into prey

Desert scorpion holding locust

Praying mantis

Powerful jaws and lightning-fast reactions make the praying mantis one of the bug world's deadliest hunters. The mantis stands perfectly still, waiting for unsuspecting prey to come within striking range of its strong fore legs.

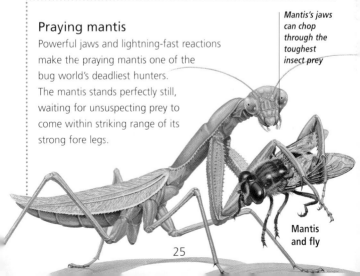

Mantis's jaws can chop through the toughest insect prey

Mantis and fly

Trap setters

Some hunting bugs go out and search for prey, relying on speed and power to catch their victims. Others use traps, tricks and lures that allow them to surprise their prey – and give them an extra split-second in which to pounce.

Antlion

The larva of the antlion is a fierce predator with spiny jaws. It sets a trap for its prey by digging a pit in sandy soil and sitting half-buried at the bottom. It tosses sand at passing ants and insects so that they fall into the pit – and into its waiting jaws.

If an ant tumbles down the pit's steep sides, it cannot escape.

Assassin bug

Some assassin bugs lure prey with scents they pick up from plants. Victims are injected with saliva. The saliva kills the prey and dissolves the victim's insides, which the bug then drinks. Assassin bugs sometimes steal prey caught in spiders' webs.

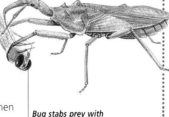

Bug stabs prey with its feeding tube

26

Trapdoor spider

The trapdoor spider ambushes its victims. Its burrow has a hinged door at the top. The spider waits inside until it senses the movement of prey overhead. Then it quickly flips up the door, grabs the prey, and hauls it down into the burrow.

Door has a hinge made of silk threads

Spider uses special spines on its jaws to dig the burrow

Spider holds the "net" with its four front legs

Net-throwing spider

This spider, also known as the ogre-faced spider, hangs from a network of dry silk threads. It holds a rectangular, sticky web, which it uses as a net to catch prey. When prey approaches, the spider stretches out the web and throws it over the passing insect. It bundles up its catch and takes it away to eat.

27

Self-defence

While many bugs are predators, bugs themselves are also hunted and eaten by other animals – including other bugs. Because of this, bugs have a wide range of self-defence methods, from stings, bites and poison sprays to playing dead.

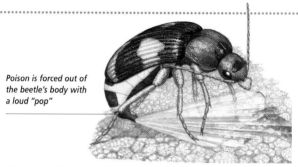

Poison is forced out of the beetle's body with a loud "pop"

Bombardier beetle

Some species of beetle use poisonous chemicals to ward off predators. If an attacker is not put off by the bombardier's bright warning colours, the beetle swivels its abdomen around to fire a spray of boiling-hot chemicals into the attacker's face.

Huge jaws make effective weapons

Army ant

Sometimes, attack is the best form of defence. The jaws of army ants are among the bug world's most impressive defence mechanisms. Platoons of army ants will attack and bite any intruder, often injuring them fatally.

Only the males have the long neck, but no one is quite sure why

Giraffe-necked weevil

This curious-looking insect gets its name from its incredibly long neck. It has an ingenious way of avoiding being eaten. If attacked, it rolls over and pretends to be dead until the danger passes. Many carnivores feed only on live flesh, so they leave the weevil alone.

Funnel-web spider

Adopting a threatening posture will sometimes deter attackers. If caught in the open, the funnel-web spider takes up an aggressive pose, raising its front legs and exposing its fearsome fangs. Some bugs, such as the cricketlike wetas, scare off enemies by making alarming noises.

Funnel-web's venom can kill a person

29

Camouflage

Bugs provide tasty meals for all kinds of other creatures. One way of avoiding being eaten by predators is to remain hidden from view, using shape and colouring to blend perfectly into the background. This is called camouflage.

Insect may let its body swing gently from side to side, like a twig being blown by the breeze

Stick insect

A stick insect's slender body is almost impossible to distinguish from a leafless twig. In daylight, it clings motionless to a plant, using its camouflage to avoid the attention of birds. At night it moves around and feeds on leaves.

Leaf insect

When this insect is sitting on a bush, its leaf-shaped wings, with veinlike markings, make it almost invisible. Even the insect's eggs resemble the seeds of the plant it lives on.

A leaf insect can also vary its colour, becoming darker at night and paler by day.

Flattened legs help to break up its outline

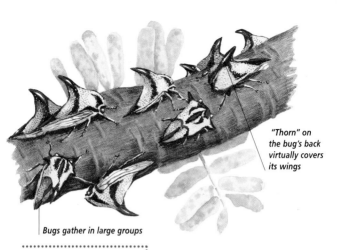

"Thorn" on the bug's back virtually covers its wings

Bugs gather in large groups

Treehopper

Hugging a branch tightly, the treehopper bug is of no interest to hungry birds. The strangely shaped extension on its thorax makes it look exactly like a thorn. It feeds mostly on plant and tree sap.

Lichen spider

The lichen spider sits head-downwards on a lichen-covered tree trunk. When danger threatens, it flattens itself against the tree bark. The spider's mottled colouring and the hairy tufts on its legs disguise it against the bark. The hairs also help to stop the spider's legs from casting noticeable shadows.

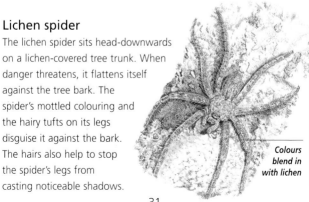

Colours blend in with lichen

31

Mimicry and warnings

Mimicking bugs avoid predators by copying the shape, colouring and behaviour of dangerous animals. Others bugs sport warning colours to tell potential predators that they are poisonous to eat.

Luna moth

The luna moth tricks birds with false-eye spots. When a predatory bird sees the flashing "eyes" on the moth's wings, it mistakes them for the eyes of one of its own enemies and backs off. The moth's trailing tails also help to protect it. They break off if it is caught, giving the moth time to escape.

Spots resemble staring eyes

Saddleback caterpillar

A plump, slow-moving caterpillar makes a tempting snack for a passing bird. Rather than using camouflage to hide from predators, the saddleback caterpillar declares its presence with a colourful patch on its back. This warns birds that it is poisonous, and thus best left alone.

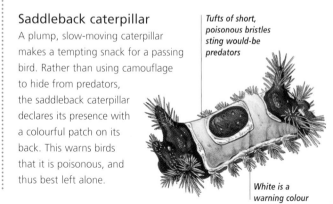

Tufts of short, poisonous bristles sting would-be predators

White is a warning colour

Colourful antennae

To a predator, the bright yellow bands say: "This bug tastes horrible"

Toxic oil beetle

The wing cases of this beetle secrete a foul-tasting oil that protects it from predators. The oil contains cantharidin, a substance that causes blisters (which is why oil beetles are also called blister beetles). Cantharidin is extracted from oil beetles and used in medicine.

Hoverfly

Potential predators often mistake this yellow-and-black striped fly for an aggressive wasp, and steer clear to avoid its venomous sting. The hoverfly is actually harmless, but it mimics the colouring and shape of wasps to fool predators. It is an expert flier, and can hover with ease and even fly backwards.

Hoverfly has only one pair of wings, whereas a wasp has two

Hoverfly feeding on flower pollen

Finding a mate

Like other animals, male and female bugs mate to produce young. Many bugs use scent to find mates of the right species, but others use sounds, displays, lights or gifts.

Glow-worm beetles

While many bugs use chemical signals to attract mates, glow-worms use light. Male glow-worms fly through the night sky flashing lights from their abdomens to attract females. A female signals her readiness to mate by flashing back. Each glow-worm species has its own distinctive pattern of flashing.

A glow-worm beetle flashes on a branch in Malaysia.

Beetle tries to lock the other in its jaws

Stag beetles

Male bugs will sometimes fight with each other over the right to mate with a female. Rival male stag beetles battle with their large, antlerlike jaws. The larger beetle usually wins by flipping its rival on to its back. The loser finds it hard to get upright again.

Dragonflies

When dragonflies mate, the male grips the neck of the female with the tip of his abdomen. The female then bends her own abdomen up, forming a heart shape. She collects sperm from the lower part of his abdomen to fertilise her eggs.

The pair mates either at rest or in flight

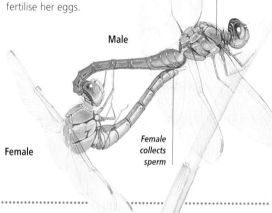

Male

Female

Female collects sperm

Spiders

A female spider attracts a male using a scent called a pheromone. To avoid being mistaken for prey and eaten by the female, a male spider may pluck at her web or perform a dance. Other males offer gifts of food or tie the female up.

A male orb weaver (left) mates with a female (right) in her web.

35

Eggs and egg laying

After mating, bugs lay their eggs. These eggs will hatch into the next generation, so they need protecting from predators. A young bug develops inside its egg until it is ready to hatch.

Damselflies

Many bugs, such as damselflies, lay their eggs in or close to water. Soon after she has mated, a female damselfly positions herself on the stem of a water plant and deposits her eggs below the waterline. The male, still flying, guards her and holds her steady while she is egg-laying.

Male grips female with his abdomen

Female

Queen and worker ant

Carpenter ant

Ants live in vast, well-organised groups called colonies. Most of the ants in the colony are female worker ants. Each colony includes a queen ant, who lays all the eggs after mating with the few male ants in the colony. Worker ants tend the eggs in special nest chambers.

Worker removes egg laid by queen

Ovipositor, or egg-laying tube

Ichneumon wasp

Bug parents often ensure
that their young will have
a ready-meal to hand when
they hatch out. The female ichneumon
wasp listens for the vibrations of a wood-
boring beetle larva in a tree trunk. She
drills into the wood with her egg-laying
tube and lays an egg on the body of the
larva. The newly hatched ichneumon will
feed on the juicy larva.

*Ovipositor is
longer than the
ichneumon's
entire body*

A female spider carrying her large white egg-sac to protect it.

Spider egg-sacs

Spiders lay their eggs and then envelop them in silk to form an
egg-sac, which may be attached to a leaf or other surface. In some
species the egg-sac contains just one egg, in others it holds as
many as 3,000. The female guards her eggs until they hatch.

Young bugs

Young bugs are tiny and vulnerable. Relatively few bug species look after their newborn young, which usually have to fend for themselves. Many perish soon after birth.

Centruroides scorpion

Scorpions do not lay eggs, but give birth to living young. Some female scorpions fold one or more pairs of legs under their bodies to form a "birth basket" that catches the young as they are born. The newborn scorpions climb up the female's legs and on to her back. She carries them around like this for a few weeks while they grow.

Froghopper nymph covered in "cuckoo spit"

Frothy mass hides nymph from predators

Froghopper nymph

The "cuckoo spit" found on plants is really a bubbly secretion produced by the nymph of the froghopper, a soft-bodied, plant-eating bug rather like an aphid. The bubbly secretion stops the nymph's body from drying out and protects it from parasites and predators.

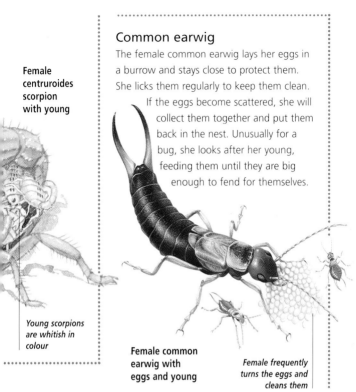

Female centruroides scorpion with young

Common earwig

The female common earwig lays her eggs in a burrow and stays close to protect them. She licks them regularly to keep them clean. If the eggs become scattered, she will collect them together and put them back in the nest. Unusually for a bug, she looks after her young, feeding them until they are big enough to fend for themselves.

Young scorpions are whitish in colour

Female common earwig with eggs and young

Female frequently turns the eggs and cleans them

Spiderlings

Many spiderlings (baby spiders) have an egg tooth to help them break out of the egg. They stay in the egg-sac for a while, feeding on the store of egg yolk inside their bodies. After they emerge, they stay together for a few days before dispersing.

A female wolf spider and spiderlings.

39

Metamorphosis

Insects go through several distinct growth stages before they become fully developed adults. This process is known as metamorphosis.

Developing wing buds

Long lower lip shoots out to grab prey

Dragonfly nymph

Incomplete metamorphosis

The young of some insects, such as dragonflies, termites, true bugs and cockroaches, are called nymphs. They hatch from eggs and look progressively more like adults each time they shed their skins. This gradual transformation from young to adult is called incomplete metamorphosis.

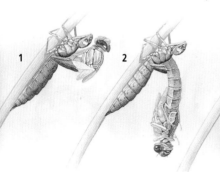

1 2 3

Skin of nymph splits and head and thorax of adult emerge

The soft-bodied adult wriggles out of the old skin

Adult waits for its wings and body to strengthen before flying away

40

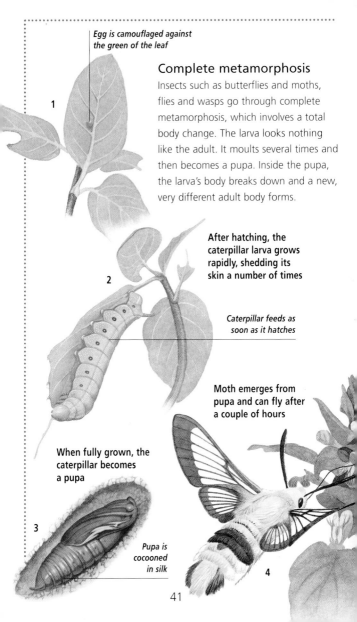

Egg is camouflaged against the green of the leaf

1

Complete metamorphosis

Insects such as butterflies and moths, flies and wasps go through complete metamorphosis, which involves a total body change. The larva looks nothing like the adult. It moults several times and then becomes a pupa. Inside the pupa, the larva's body breaks down and a new, very different adult body forms.

After hatching, the caterpillar larva grows rapidly, shedding its skin a number of times

2

Caterpillar feeds as soon as it hatches

Moth emerges from pupa and can fly after a couple of hours

When fully grown, the caterpillar becomes a pupa

3

Pupa is cocooned in silk

4

Social insects

Some bugs, such as termites, bees, ants and wasps, live in huge groups called colonies. Usually, a single female queen lays all the eggs, while worker insects run the colony.

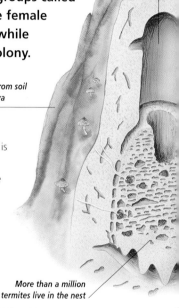

"Chimney" lets air in and out and regulates the temperature inside

Mound is built from soil and termite saliva

More than a million termites live in the nest

Termite mound

Of all bug nests, a termite mound is the most spectacular, rising up to nearly 5 metres (16 feet) high. The interior is a maze of tunnels and chambers. Some chambers are food stores, others are nurseries for tending eggs and young, and there is even a royal chamber for the queen termite – the head of the colony.

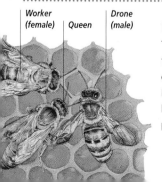

Worker (female) *Queen* *Drone (male)*

Bee honeycomb

The honeybee builds its nest from wax that it makes in its own body. The nest consists of sheets of hexagonal cells. Each sheet is called a comb. Eggs are laid in some cells and food, such as pollen or honey, is stored in others.

42

Termites grow fungi to eat

Paper wasp nest

A queen paper wasp builds a nest on her own. She makes a series of papery envelopes out of chewed-up wood mixed with saliva. She then lays her eggs in the envelopes. Later, other females arrive to help her feed her newly hatched larvae with insects.

Nest usually contains about 20 wasps

There is no outer covering to the nest, and the egg cells are open to the air

Developing larvae

Weaver ants

These ants make nests in trees. Worker ants pull two leaves together. Others hold ant larvae in their jaws and stimulate them to produce silk, which the ants use to "sew" the leaf edges together. The finished nest is a ball or column of leaves.

Weaver ants at work.

Bugs that Glow

Some bugs have developed the amazing ability to glow in the dark. Chemical reactions inside their bodies produce light, which the bugs use to attract mates, lure prey, or ward off attackers.

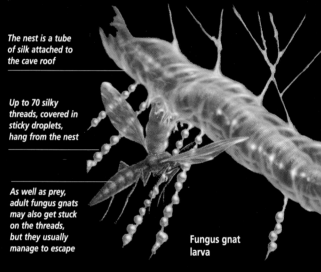

The nest is a tube of silk attached to the cave roof

Up to 70 silky threads, covered in sticky droplets, hang from the nest

As well as prey, adult fungus gnats may also get stuck on the threads, but they usually manage to escape

Fungus gnat larva

Fungus Gnat

The fungus gnat is a flylike insect. Lying in a tubular nest that hangs from a cave ceiling, a fungus gnat larva makes the tip of its abdomen glow to lure prey such as midges and moths. The insects fly towards the light and become trapped on the sticky threads that dangle from the nest.

Railroad Beetle

The adult female or larva of the railroad beetle looks very like a worm. If threatened while hunting at night, it scares away its attacker by suddenly switching on its glowing body-lights, which resemble the windows of a night train.

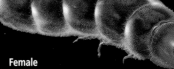

Head glows a bright red and its body a pale, greenish-yellow

Female

Female Glow-Worm

A female glow-worm beetle is wingless. At dusk, she crawls up a grass stem and waves her glowing abdomen in the air to attract a male flying by. Some glow-worms use their lights in self-defence, flashing them to warn predators that they taste unpleasant.

Larva shines its light onto the threads to make them glitter

Yellowish-green light is produced on the underside of the abdomen

Female glow-worm

Bug migrations

While some bugs spend their whole lives in one place, others travel far and wide each year to find a better climate or good supplies of food. These journeys are known as migrations.

Airborne spiders

Spiders lack wings, but they are not earthbound. To avoid overcrowding or competition for limited food supplies, many spiders "balloon". This involves spinning a short length of silk, which is caught by the breeze and carries the spider through the air.

Ballooning spiders

Painted lady butterfly

Each spring, painted ladies travel over 1,000 kilometres (600 miles), from Africa to northern Europe and from Mexico to Canada. As well as avoiding the hottest summer temperatures, it is probably also a way for the butterfly to spread the species' population over a wider area.

Painted ladies travel huge distances on relatively simple wings.

Desert locusts

If their numbers become too great or food becomes scarce, desert locusts will migrate to find new feeding areas. They fly in swarms, often numbering many millions, devouring farm crops as they move from place to place.

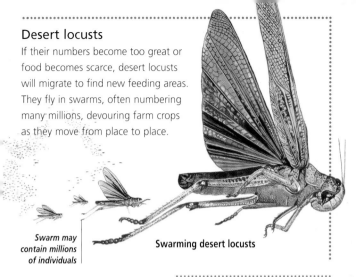

Swarm may contain millions of individuals

Swarming desert locusts

Hoverfly

Bean aphid

Aphid and hoverfly

Huge swarms of hoverflies sometimes move hundreds of kilometres to find new feeding areas. They are a welcome sight in gardens, because their young eat aphids, which damage many garden plants.

Army ants

Unlike most ants, army ants do not build permanent nests but are constantly on the move in search of prey. They travel in vast columns of up to 750,000 ants, eating anything in their path.

Army ants on the move.

Water bugs

The world's ponds, lakes and streams are home to more than 2,000 different species of true bug. Some are so light they can walk on the water's surface, while others are excellent divers.

Giant water bug

Measuring up to 15 centimetres (6 inches) long, the giant water bug is the largest of the true bugs. Its streamlined shape makes this strong swimmer a superb underwater hunter. It lives in slow-moving water, preferring the muddy bottoms of ponds and lakes.

Large eyes

Large front legs shoot out to seize prey

Boat-shaped body

Water boatman

Unlike most water bugs, water boatmen are not carnivorous predators, but feed on plants and algae. Like the giant water bugs, they swim with their middle and back legs. They use their scooplike front legs for collecting food, which they sift out of the silt.

Short front legs

Flat, oval body helps bug move easily through the water

Bug swims with its powerful middle and back legs

Backswimmer

This fierce predator swims upside down, just below the surface, seizing insects and small creatures. Like other true bugs that live in water, it traps air under its wings. It uses this to breathe under-water through abdominal openings called spiracles.

Hairy fringes on legs give buoyancy

Long, oar-shaped back legs enable the backswimmer to move rapidly through the water

Water measurer

With its long legs and water-repellent feet, the water measurer strides slowly over the surface of a pond. It feeds mostly on dead and dying insects, but also spears water fleas with its piercing mouthparts and sucks out its victims' body fluids.

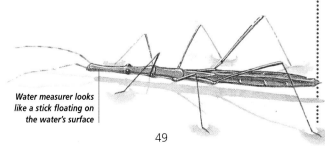

Water measurer looks like a stick floating on the water's surface

Guide to bugs

A yellow mass of baby garden spiders starts to disperse along strands of silk when danger threatens.

Cockroaches, earwigs and bristletails

Cockroaches are familiar but unwelcome guests in our homes. Also found in homes are the wingless insects called bristletails. Earwigs usually live outdoors, often in gardens.

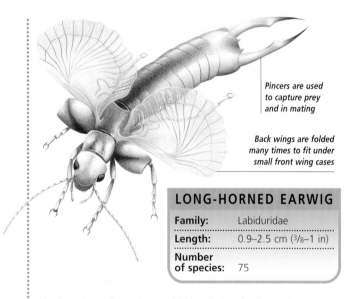

Pincers are used to capture prey and in mating

Back wings are folded many times to fit under small front wing cases

LONG-HORNED EARWIG

Family:	Labiduridae
Length:	0.9–2.5 cm (^{3}/8–1 in)
Number of species:	75

The long-horned earwig stays hidden during the day and emerges at night to hunt other insects. If attacked, the earwig squirts a bad-smelling liquid from special glands on its abdomen.

SILVERFISH

Family:	Lepismatidae
Length:	0.8–1.9 cm ($\frac{1}{3}$–$\frac{3}{4}$ in)
Number of species:	200

Long, tapering body is covered in silvery scales

The silverfish is a bristletail. It usually lives in houses, hiding from the light in dark corners. Silverfish feed on starchy materials such as paper, glue and spilled flour.

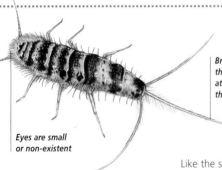

Bristletails have three slender "tails" at the hind end of their abdomen

Eyes are small or non-existent

FIREBRAT

Family:	Lepismatidae
Length:	0.8–1.9 cm ($\frac{1}{3}$–$\frac{3}{4}$ in)
Number of species:	200

Like the silverfish, the firebrat is a house-dwelling bristletail. It gets its name because it likes to live near the warmth of boilers, fires or ovens. It scurries about looking for scraps of food and other debris to eat.

AMERICAN COCKROACH

Family:	Blattidae
Length:	1.9–5 cm (3/4–2 in)
Number of species:	600

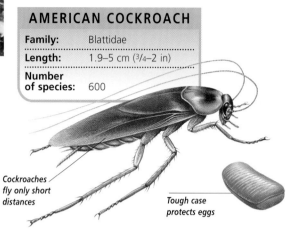

Cockroaches fly only short distances

Tough case protects eggs

American cockroaches hide by day and feed at night on anything they can find. The female lays her eggs in a case attached to her body. She leaves it in a dark, safe place until the eggs hatch.

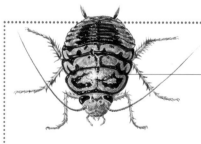

Striking wing cases are shining brown-black, marbled with yellow

HARLEQUIN COCKROACH

Family:	Blattidae
Length:	1.9–5 cm (3/4–2 in)
Number of species:	600

Harlequin cockroaches live in Malaysia, where they are often found in houses. Like other cockroaches, they can breed rapidly: a female lays a new egg case roughly every 3 days throughout her life.

Long, sensitive antennae

Flattened body is ideal for squeezing into cracks and under floorboards

GERMAN COCKROACH

Family:	Blattellidae
Length:	0.6–2.5 cm (¼–1 in)
Number of species:	1,750

Although cockroaches live in almost every habitat on Earth, German cockroaches are usually found indoors. They can spread disease by walking over food with feet that are dirty from sewers and drains.

MADAGASCAN HISSING COCKROACH

Family:	Blaberidae
Length:	5–7.5 cm (2–3 in)
Number of species:	1,000

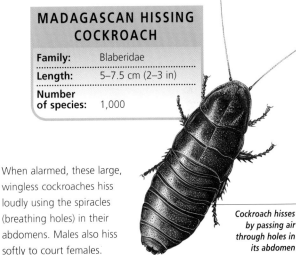

When alarmed, these large, wingless cockroaches hiss loudly using the spiracles (breathing holes) in their abdomens. Males also hiss softly to court females.

Cockroach hisses by passing air through holes in its abdomen

Crickets, grasshoppers and relatives

Grasshoppers and crickets are best known for the calls made by the males during courtship, using special parts of their legs or wings.

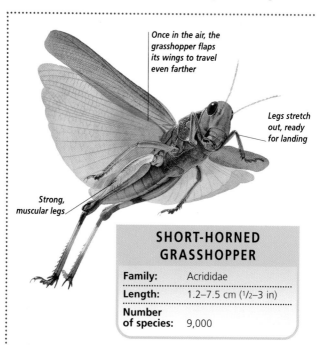

Once in the air, the grasshopper flaps its wings to travel even farther

Legs stretch out, ready for landing

Strong, muscular legs

SHORT-HORNED GRASSHOPPER

Family:	Acrididae
Length:	1.2–7.5 cm (1/2–3 in)
Number of species:	9,000

Short-horned grasshoppers have short antennae. Like all grasshoppers, they have powerful back legs. They can leap more than 200 times their own length to escape from danger.

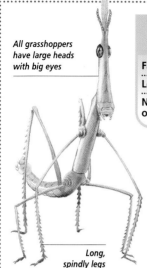

All grasshoppers have large heads with big eyes

Long, spindly legs

FALSE STICK INSECT

Family:	Proscopiidae
Length:	up to 10 cm (4 in)
Number of species:	150

The bizarre-looking false stick insect is really a grasshopper that fools its enemies into mistaking it for an inedible stick. False stick insects live in trees, bushes and low-growing plants in tropical rainforests and semi-desert areas.

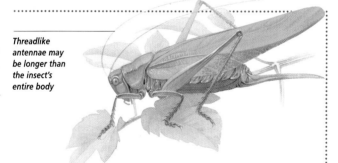

Threadlike antennae may be longer than the insect's entire body

LONG-HORNED GRASSHOPPER

Family:	Tettigoniidae
Length:	1.2–7.5 cm (1/2–3 in)
Number of species:	5,000

These grasshoppers emerge at dusk to eat plants and prey on small insects. It takes 40–60 days and several moults for a young grasshopper to become an adult.

LOCUST

Family:	Acrididae
Length:	1.2–7.5 cm (1/2–3 in)
Number of species:	9,000

Tough, narrow fore wings

Delicate hind wings

A female locust has short, hooked "blades" on her ovipositor (egg-laying tube) to dig into the soil. She lays a pod of eggs in the ground and then fills in the hole to hide the eggs from parasites.

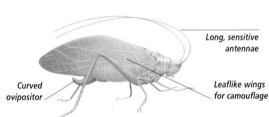

Long, sensitive antennae

Curved ovipositor

Leaflike wings for camouflage

KATYDID

Family:	Tettigoniidae
Length:	1.2–7.5 cm (1/2–3 in)
Number of species:	5,000

The katydid gets its name from its song, which sounds like "katy-did, katy-didn't", chirped repeatedly. The female has a knifelike ovipositor. She uses this to cut slots in plant stems, in which she lays her eggs.

Fine hairs protect the body from soil

Large, spadelike fore legs with sharp claws

MOLE CRICKET

Family:	Gryllotalpidae
Length:	2–5 cm (¾–2 in)
Number of species:	60

Like a tiny mole, this insect spends its life underground, feeding on plant roots, worms and larvae. It uses its powerful fore legs for burrowing through the soil.

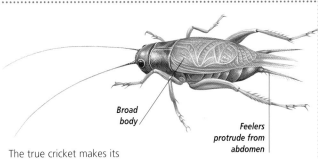

Broad body

Feelers protrude from abdomen

The true cricket makes its high-pitched call by rubbing together veins and ridges on its fore wings. It has "ears" just below the knees on its fore legs, to pick up the mating songs of other crickets.

TRUE CRICKET

Family:	Gryllidae
Length:	0.9–2.5 cm (⅜–1 in)
Number of species:	2,000

Mantids, dragonflies and relatives

Mantids snatch victims with lightning-fast movements of their fore legs. Dragonflies are flying hunters that pluck prey out of the air.

The praying mantis gets its name from the way it often holds its front legs together like a person at prayer. The females are known for attacking or even eating males during mating.

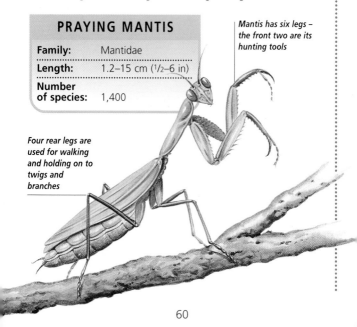

PRAYING MANTIS

Family:	Mantidae
Length:	1.2–15 cm (1/2–6 in)
Number of species:	1,400

Mantis has six legs – the front two are its hunting tools

Four rear legs are used for walking and holding on to twigs and branches

FLOWER MANTIS

Family:	Mantidae
Length:	1.2–15 cm (1/2–6 in)
Number of species:	1,400

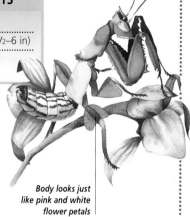

The pink flower mantis looks just like the tropical orchid flower on which it feeds. Like other mantises, it waits patient and still, until an insect comes close. It snaps the prey up and eats it alive.

Body looks just like pink and white flower petals

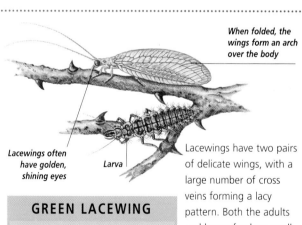

When folded, the wings form an arch over the body

Lacewings often have golden, shining eyes

Larva

GREEN LACEWING

Family:	Chrysopidae
Length:	0.9–1.9 cm (3/8–3/4 in)
Number of species:	1,600

Lacewings have two pairs of delicate wings, with a large number of cross veins forming a lacy pattern. Both the adults and larvae feed on small insects such as aphids. The larvae have long, tubular jaws for sucking the body contents from their prey.

Mobile head

MANTISFLY

Family:	Mantispidae
Length:	0.3–2.5 cm (1/8–1 in)
Number of species:	350

Mantisfly hunts by snatching prey with its fore legs, just like a praying mantis

Grasping fore legs, a long thorax and large eyes make this relative of the lacewing resemble a small praying mantis. Mantisfly larvae are parasitic, feeding on bee and wasp larvae or spider eggs.

Dragonflies beat their wings up to 20 times a second

CLUBTAIL DRAGONFLY

Family:	Gomphidae
Length:	5–7.5 cm (2–6 in)
Number of species:	875

Thick, clublike end to abdomen

While most dragonflies hunt on the wing as they fly to and fro over water, clubtails and darters prefer to wait on a sunlit perch for prey to pass by. When the clubtail spots the prey, it dashes out to seize it, then returns to its warm perch.

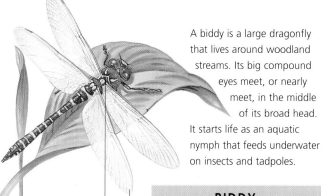

A biddy is a large dragonfly that lives around woodland streams. Its big compound eyes meet, or nearly meet, in the middle of its broad head. It starts life as an aquatic nymph that feeds underwater on insects and tadpoles.

Fine hairs cover head and thorax

Dragonfly holds its wings horizontally when it is at rest on a leaf or stem

BIDDY

Family:	Cordulegastridae
Length:	6–8.5 cm (2½–3¼ in)
Number of species:	75

EMPEROR DRAGONFLY

Family:	Aeschnidae
Length:	6–12 cm (2½–4¾ in)
Number of species:	about 1,000

Wings are up to 12.5 cm (5 in) long

Like many dragonflies, a male emperor usually establishes a territory (a stretch of land or water) that he patrols and defends. He allows female mates to enter the territory, but chases away rival males.

63

Adult mayflies do not feed, and may live for only a few hours. This gives them just enough time to mate and lay their eggs. Mayfly nymphs, however, live in water for a year or more before becoming winged adults.

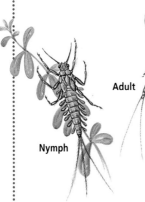

Slender body and large, flimsy wings

Adult

Nymph

MAYFLY

Family:	Baetidae
Length:	about 1 cm (³/₈ in)
Number of species:	800

SKIMMER

Family:	Libellulidae
Length:	2–6 cm (³/₄–2¹/₂ in)
Number of species:	1,250

Skimmers have a wingspan of up to 10 cm (4 in)

This wide-bodied dragonfly is often seen flying near still or slow-moving water, such as ponds or swamps. Like other dragonflies, it does not move around much when perched on plants or rocks, because it cannot fold back its long wings.

Many darters spend much of their time sunbathing on rocks or plants

Darter dragonflies get their name because of their quick, darting flight. Some female darters dip their abdomens in the water to lay eggs, while others glue their eggs to rocks or plants above the surface or flick them on to the riverbank.

DARTER

Family:	Libellulidae
Length:	2–6 cm (³/₄–2¹/₂ in)
Number of species:	1,250

Eyes are further apart than those of dragonflies, giving the head a dumb-bell appearance

At rest, wings are either vertical or slightly spread out

Most damselflies are more delicately built than dragonflies, with thinner bodies and weaker, more fluttering flight. Damselflies live around ponds and marshes, where they prey on aphids and other small insects.

DAMSELFLY

Family:	Lestidae
Length:	3–5 cm (1¹/₄–2 in)
Number of species:	200

Bugs, lice and fleas

Although bug is a general term for insects and spiders, it also refers to a particular group of insects. "True bugs" include cicadas and aphids. Lice and fleas are parasitic insects.

CICADA

Family:	Cicadidae
Length:	up to 5 cm (2 in)
Number of species:	2,500

Adult cicada emerging from nymph skin

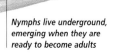

Nymphs live underground, emerging when they are ready to become adults

The cicada is known for the shrill call made by the males. The noise is made by drumlike structures called tymbals on the male's abdomen. Like other true bugs, it has needlelike mouthparts for piercing food and sucking out the contents. Cicadas feed on plant sap.

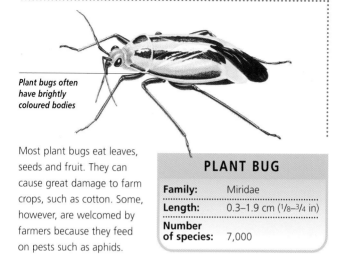

Plant bugs often have brightly coloured bodies

Most plant bugs eat leaves, seeds and fruit. They can cause great damage to farm crops, such as cotton. Some, however, are welcomed by farmers because they feed on pests such as aphids.

PLANT BUG

Family:	Miridae
Length:	0.3–1.9 cm (1/8–3/4 in)
Number of species:	7,000

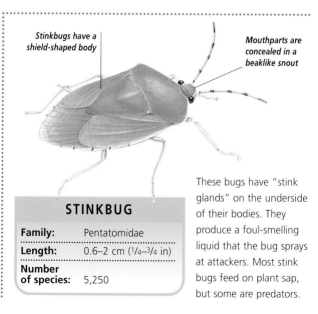

Stinkbugs have a shield-shaped body

Mouthparts are concealed in a beaklike snout

STINKBUG

Family:	Pentatomidae
Length:	0.6–2 cm (1/4–3/4 in)
Number of species:	5,250

These bugs have "stink glands" on the underside of their bodies. They produce a foul-smelling liquid that the bug sprays at attackers. Most stink bugs feed on plant sap, but some are predators.

Lying hidden during the day, bedbugs come out at night to feed on the blood of birds and mammals. Unlike fleas and lice, they do not live on their host's body, but in the home or nest of the host animal.

BEDBUG

Family:	Cimicidae
Length:	up to 0.6 cm (1/4 in)
Number of species:	90

Flat body makes it easy for the flea to hide in crevices and small gaps.

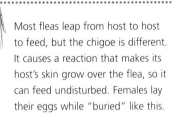

Most fleas leap from host to host to feed, but the chigoe is different. It causes a reaction that makes its host's skin grow over the flea, so it can feed undisturbed. Females lay their eggs while "buried" like this.

CHIGOE FLEA

Family:	Tungidae
Length:	0.3–0.6 cm (1/8–1/4 in)
Number of species:	20

FEATHER LOUSE

Family:	Philopteridae
Length:	0.15 cm (1/16 in)
Number of species:	2,700

The feather louse is a chewing louse that lives and feeds on the feathers of a wide range of birds. The female louse lays up to 100 eggs, which she fixes to the feathers with a gluey liquid produced by her own body.

Louse bites off pieces of feather with its jaws

Eggs are attached to hairs of human host

HEAD LOUSE

Family:	Pediculidae
Length:	0.15–0.3 cm (1/16–1/8 in)
Number of species:	2

The head louse is a sucking louse, which means that it feeds on its human host by piercing the skin of the scalp with its mouthparts and sucking up the blood. The head louse stays on its host by holding on to hairs with its claws and strong legs.

Beetles

There are more than 300,000 species of beetle around the world. Most beetles have two pairs of wings. The front pair are hard and act as covers for the more delicate back wings.

GOLIATH BEETLE

Family:	Scarabaeidae
Length:	1.8–18 cm (³/4–7 in)
Number of species:	20,000

Strong front legs make the goliath an excellent climber

One of the world's largest flying insects, the African goliath beetle weighs up to 100 g (3¹/2 oz). Females are smaller than males and not so brightly patterned. Adults feed on the fruit or sap of trees. They mate in the treetops but lay their eggs on the ground. Their larvae live in rotting vegetation.

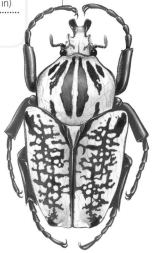

Male goliath beetle

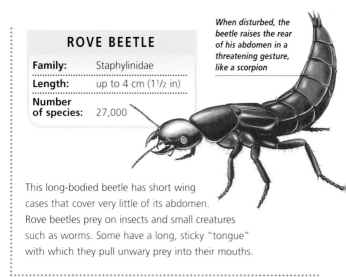

ROVE BEETLE

Family:	Staphylinidae
Length:	up to 4 cm (1½ in)
Number of species:	27,000

When disturbed, the beetle raises the rear of his abdomen in a threatening gesture, like a scorpion

This long-bodied beetle has short wing cases that cover very little of its abdomen. Rove beetles prey on insects and small creatures such as worms. Some have a long, sticky "tongue" with which they pull unwary prey into their mouths.

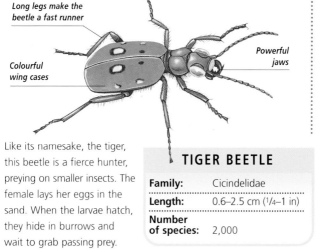

Long legs make the beetle a fast runner

Colourful wing cases

Powerful jaws

Like its namesake, the tiger, this beetle is a fierce hunter, preying on smaller insects. The female lays her eggs in the sand. When the larvae hatch, they hide in burrows and wait to grab passing prey.

TIGER BEETLE

Family:	Cicindelidae
Length:	0.6–2.5 cm (¼–1 in)
Number of species:	2,000

WHIRLIGIG BEETLE

Family:	Gyrinidae
Length:	0.3–1.5 cm ($^1/_8$–$^5/_8$ in)
Number of species:	750

Wing cases are glossy and black

Whirligigs may hunt alone or gather in groups

Whirligigs spin round on the water's surface as they hunt for insects that have fallen into the water. Their eyes have two parts, so they can see above and below the surface at the same time.

Paddling quickly with its hind legs, the diving beetle is the fastest underwater insect. Both adults and larvae are voracious predators, attacking virtually anything edible, including fish and tadpoles. Adults sometimes fly from one pond to another.

Adult

Larva

Defenceless tadpoles are easy prey for the fierce larva

DIVING BEETLE

Family:	Dytiscidae
Length:	0.15–4 cm ($^1/_{16}$–$1^1/_2$ in)
Number of species:	3,500

COLORADO BEETLE

Family:	Chrysomelidae
Length:	up to 1.6 cm (3/5 in)
Number of species:	20,000

The beetle's yellowish back has 10 black stripes along it

The Colorado beetle is a leaf eater. It is much feared by farmers, as adults and larvae can devastate potato plants, quickly reducing them to a blackened mess. It can be controlled with pesticides.

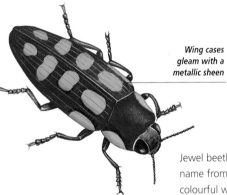

Wing cases gleam with a metallic sheen

JEWEL BEETLE

Family:	Buprestidae
Length:	2–6 cm (3/4–2 1/2 in)
Number of species:	14,000

Jewel beetles get their name from their bright, colourful wing cases. They feed on the flower nectar and leaves of tropical trees. Jewel beetle larvae feed by boring into dead and living wood, so they are often considered pests.

Long antennae have about 10 jointed segments and are up to three times the length of the beetle's body

Small eyes

LONGHORN BEETLE

Family:	Cerambycidae
Length:	up to 18 cm (7 in)
Number of species:	25,000

Clawed feet

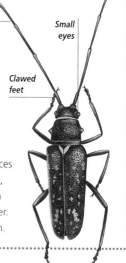

A female longhorn lays her eggs in crevices in trees and logs. When the larvae hatch, they tunnel into the wood to feed, often causing great damage to trees and timber. Adults feed mainly on flowers and pollen.

SCARAB BEETLE

Family:	Scarabaeidae
Length:	1.8–18 cm (¾–7 in)
Number of species:	20,000

Scarab beetles are usually stout and heavy-bodied

Scarabs are dung beetles. They roll animal dung into balls, bury the balls and eat them at leisure. After mating, the female lays an egg in the centre of a dung ball. The dung is the food for the newly hatched larvae.

CARRION BEETLE

Family:	Silphidae
Length:	up to 4 cm (1½ in)
Number of species:	250

Most carrion beetles feed on dead animals, such as mice and birds. Some will lay eggs on a dead creature and then bury it, so that their young have a ready supply of food. They are also called undertaker beetles.

Hind part of abdomen is exposed

The weevil bores into buds and seedpods using jaws at the end of its long snout

Weevils are plant-eating beetles. Boll weevils can cause serious crop damage as they feed on the buds and seedpods (bolls) of cotton plants. The female lays her eggs in holes drilled into the seedpods.

BOLL WEEVIL

Family:	Curculionidae
Length:	0.15–4 cm (1/16–1½ in)
Number of species:	40,000

With its long horns, a rhinoceros beetle can lift up to 850 times its own weight. In the mating season, it uses its horns as weapons in fights with rival males over females.

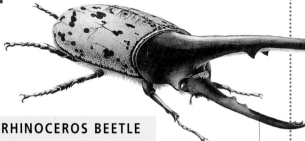

RHINOCEROS BEETLE

Family:	Scarabaeidae
Length:	1.8–12.5 cm (³/4–5 in)
Number of species:	20,000

Horns have spiny hairs to help grip rivals and slam them down on their backs

DARKLING BEETLE

Family:	Tenebrionidae
Length:	2–4.5 cm (³/4–1³/4 in)
Number of species:	15,000

These beetles are common in dry areas. They lurk in shadows under stones during the day, hidden by their dark colouring. They scavenge for food at night.

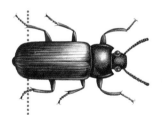

From above, the beetle's flat body looks violin-shaped

CLICK BEETLE

Family:	Elateridae
Length:	up to 6 cm (2½ in)
Number of species:	8,500

When turned on their backs, these beetles right themselves by suddenly leaping into the air with a loud click. They can jump as high as 30 cm (11¾ in).

A ladybird's colourful body warns that it tastes unpleasant and may be poisonous. Ladybirds feed mostly on aphids. They often hibernate in winter, clustering together in sheltered hollows.

LADYBIRD

Family:	Coccinellidae
Length:	up to 0.9 cm (⅜ in)
Number of species:	5,000

Little is known about this strange-looking beetle. Its flattened body enables it to live wedged between layers of bracket fungi on the trunks of forest trees in Indonesia.

VIOLIN BEETLE

Family:	Mormolyce phyllodes
Length:	0.15–4 cm (1/16–1½ in)
Number of species:	25,000

Flies, moths and butterflies

Butterflies and moths have two pairs of wings covered in tiny scales. Flies have only one pair of wings, but they are more agile in the air. All are important pollinators of plants.

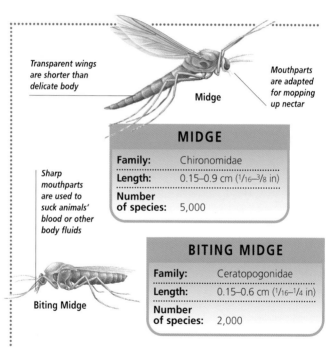

Transparent wings are shorter than delicate body

Midge

Mouthparts are adapted for mopping up nectar

Sharp mouthparts are used to suck animals' blood or other body fluids

MIDGE

Family:	Chironomidae
Length:	0.15–0.9 cm (¹/₁₆–³/₈ in)
Number of species:	5,000

Biting Midge

BITING MIDGE

Family:	Ceratopogonidae
Length:	0.15–0.6 cm (¹/₁₆–¹/₄ in)
Number of species:	2,000

Swarms of tiny midges gather on warm evenings near ponds and lakes. There are two midge families. Ceratopogonidae midges bite animals, including humans. Non-biting Chironomidae midges feed on nectar, and also on rotting plants and algae. Some are predators.

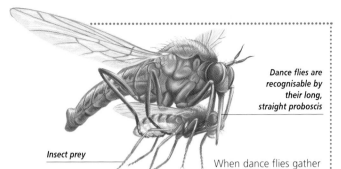

Dance flies are recognisable by their long, straight proboscis

Insect prey

DANCE FLY

Family:	Empididae
Length:	up to 0.9 cm (³/₈ in)
Number of species:	3,500

When dance flies gather in swarms, they bob up and down in a dancelike flight. Females normally feed on flowers, but males hunt small insects. During courtship, a male may present a female with a dead insect as a "wedding present".

Male horseflies feed on pollen and nectar, but females suck the blood of animals, inflicting a painful wound on victims. They are common in damp pastures where animals such as horses graze.

HORSEFLY

Family:	Tabanidae
Length:	0.6–2.5 cm (¹/₄–1 in)
Number of species:	4,100

Large eyes are an iridescent (shimmering) green

Beating wings make a loud humming noise

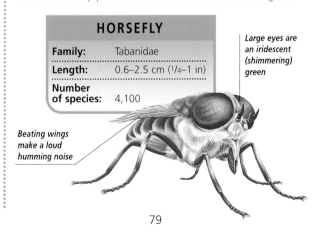

BLACK FLY

Family:	Simulidae
Length:	up to 0.6 cm (¼ in)
Number of species:	1,500

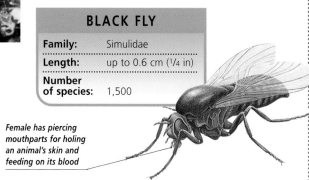

Female has piercing mouthparts for holing an animal's skin and feeding on its blood

These stout-bodied flies have a humped back, which is why they are also called buffalo flies. Males feed on flower nectar, but most females are blood suckers, taking food from mammals and birds.

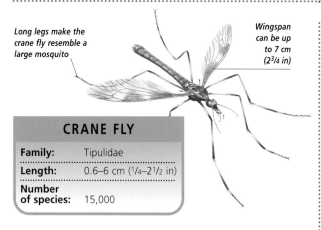

Long legs make the crane fly resemble a large mosquito

Wingspan can be up to 7 cm (2¾ in)

CRANE FLY

Family:	Tipulidae
Length:	0.6–6 cm (¼–2½ in)
Number of species:	15,000

Most adult crane flies live for a few days only, and do not eat at all. The larvae eat mainly roots and rotting plants, but some are predators. Some larvae have such tough skin they are called "leatherjackets".

HOUSEFLY

Family:	Muscidae
Length:	0.3–1.2 cm ($^1/_8$–$^1/_2$ in)
Number of species:	3,000

Houseflies are so agile in flight that they can evade most predators

Houseflies are found in homes in almost every part of the world. Their larvae, called maggots, thrive in rotting meat and rubbish. The adults can spread diseases with their feet when they walk over uncovered food.

Adults may carry germs on their feet, as they often feed on manure and decaying matter

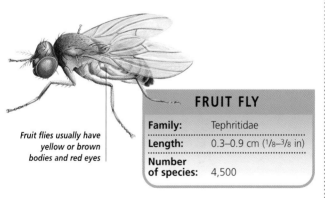

FRUIT FLY

Fruit flies usually have yellow or brown bodies and red eyes

Family:	Tephritidae
Length:	0.3–0.9 cm ($^1/_8$–$^3/_8$ in)
Number of species:	4,500

These small flies love flowers, ripe fruit and fermenting materials such as wine. The larvae develop in rotting fruit. Some fruit flies are serious pests, causing damage to orchards and other fruit crops.

The caterpillars of these small, brownish moths feed on hair and feathers, and the dried corpses of small birds and mammals. The caterpillars often come into homes to feed on clothes made of natural fibres such as wool.

CLOTHES MOTH

Family:	Tineidae
Wingspan:	0.6–2 cm (1/4–3/4 in)
Number of species:	2,500

Narrow front wings fold neatly over the body

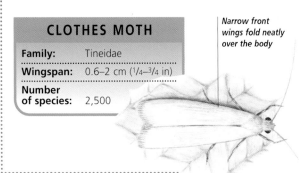

These moths have slim bodies and fragile wings. Some female geometrids are wingless. The caterpillars are known as loopers, because of the looping shapes they make as they move along. For safety, they spin a silk thread and attach it to a branch in case they fall off.

GEOMETRID MOTH

Family:	Geometridae
Wingspan:	1.2–4 cm (1/2–11/2 in)
Number of species:	18,000

Wings are spread out flat when moth is at rest

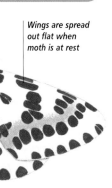

OLEANDER SPHINX MOTH

Family:	Sphingidae
Wingspan:	3–15 cm (1¼–6 in)
Number of species:	1,200

The oleander sphinx moth is one of the most delicately patterned of all moths

Sphinx moths, also called hawk moths, have heavy bodies and long, narrow wings. The fat oleander caterpillar grows up to 15 cm (6 in) long, and feeds on plants such as the shrub oleander.

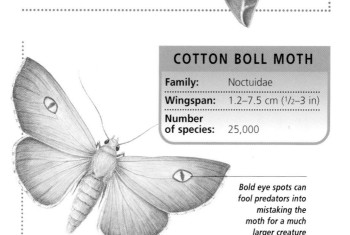

COTTON BOLL MOTH

Family:	Noctuidae
Wingspan:	1.2–7.5 cm (½–3 in)
Number of species:	25,000

Bold eye spots can fool predators into mistaking the moth for a much larger creature

This moth belongs to one of the biggest families of moths, most of which fly at night and are dull in pattern and colour. Cotton boll caterpillars eat cotton seedpods and can damage cotton plants.

SPHINX MOTH

Family:	Sphingidae
Wingspan:	3–15 cm (1¼–6 in)
Number of species:	1,200

The sphinx moth lives near the edges of woods and in parks. It is active at night and lays its eggs in poplar and willow trees. When its caterpillar is fully grown, it pupates in a hole under the ground, where it hibernates.

Colour and irregular shape of wings help to hide moth as it rests on bark during the day

TIGER MOTH

Family:	Arctiidae
Wingspan:	2–7 cm (¾–2¾ in)
Number of species:	2,500

When disturbed, the moth shows its red hind wings

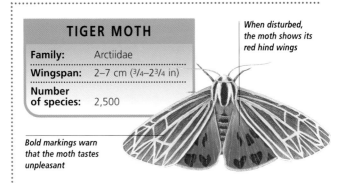

Bold markings warn that the moth tastes unpleasant

The hairy caterpillars of tiger moths feed on plants that are poisonous to vertebrate animals (those with backbones). The caterpillars store the poison in their bodies for their own protection.

These colourful moths are among the largest in the world. Most have transparent patches on their wings and feathery antennae. Their leaf-eating caterpillars are covered in a whitish powder.

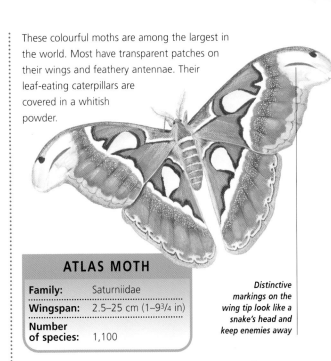

ATLAS MOTH

Family:	Saturniidae
Wingspan:	2.5–25 cm (1–9³/₄ in)
Number of species:	1,100

Distinctive markings on the wing tip look like a snake's head and keep enemies away

Found near ponds and streams, caddis flies look like moths but do not have scales on their wings or hairs on their bodies. The larvae are usually aquatic and live in cases made of leaves, twigs or stones.

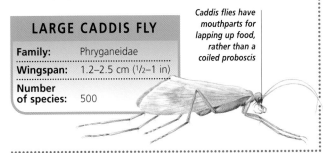

LARGE CADDIS FLY

Family:	Phryganeidae
Wingspan:	1.2–2.5 cm (¹/₂–1 in)
Number of species:	500

Caddis flies have mouthparts for lapping up food, rather than a coiled proboscis

SWALLOWTAIL

Family:	Papilionidae
Wingspan:	5–28 cm (2–11 in)
Number of species:	700

Wing "tails" distract predators away from vulnerable head area

Swallowtails get their name from the tail-like extensions to their rear wings. Swallowtails are fast fliers that live in grasslands and wetland forests. Some females lay more than 500 eggs.

FLUMINENSE SWALLOWTAIL

Family:	Papilionidae
Wingspan:	5–28 cm (2–11 in)
Number of species:	700

This striking butterfly lives in coastal swamps in South America, but it is in danger because much of its habitat is being drained for building houses and factories, and to plant crops.

Dark fore wings have a white flash down the middle

Hind wings are suffused with pink

CAIRNS BIRDWING

Family:	Papilionidae
Wingspan:	5–28 cm (2–11 in)
Number of species:	700

Birdwings are found only in Southeast Asia and northern Australia. Cairns birdwings live in the rainforest canopy and breed on vines. They are thought to be poisonous to predators such as birds.

The more colourful males are smaller than the females, which are black, white and yellow

COPPER

Family:	Lycaenidae
Wingspan:	2.5–5 cm (1–2 in)
Number of species:	6,000

Brightly coloured, iridescent wings

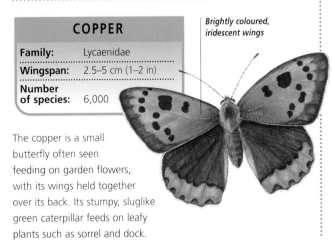

The copper is a small butterfly often seen feeding on garden flowers, with its wings held together over its back. Its stumpy, sluglike green caterpillar feeds on leafy plants such as sorrel and dock.

Each autumn, millions of monarchs migrate 3,200 km (2,000 miles) from Canada to Mexico, returning north the following spring. Like all Nymphalid butterflies, monarchs walk on four legs – the front pair is too small to be used for walking.

MONARCH

Family:	Nymphalidae
Wingspan:	2.5–11 cm (1–4¼ in)
Number of species:	3,500

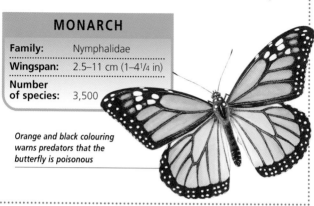

Orange and black colouring warns predators that the butterfly is poisonous

Male morphos are among the world's most spectacular butterflies. Females are much plainer. They live in tropical rainforests and feed on the juices of rotting fruit and sap seeping from damaged trees.

MORPHO

Family:	Nymphalidae
Wingspan:	2.5–11 cm (1–4¼ in)
Number of species:	3,500

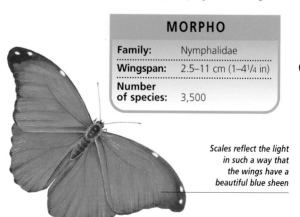

Scales reflect the light in such a way that the wings have a beautiful blue sheen

CABBAGE WHITE

Family:	Pieridae
Wingspan:	0.9–7 cm (3/4–2 3/4 in)
Number of species:	1,300

Unlike many butterflies, cabbage whites have well-developed front legs, which they use for walking. Adults feed on nectar, but the caterpillars eat leafy crops such as cabbages and radishes.

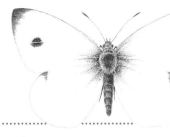

Males have one black spot on each fore wing; females have two

QUEEN ALEXANDRA'S BIRDWING

Family:	Papilionidae
Wingspan:	5–28 cm (2–11 in)
Number of species:	700

Wingspan is an incredible 28 cm (11 in), greater than any other butterfly

With its uniquely shaped wings, the Queen Alexandra's birdwing is the largest butterfly in the world. It lives high in the treetops, but is in danger of extinction because the rainforests in which it lives are gradually being cut down.

Bright yellow abdomen

Bees, wasps, ants and termites

Bees, ants and wasps have a narrow "waist" and tonguelike structures for sucking up liquid. Termites live in huge colonies in soil or trees.

BUMBLEBEE

Family:	Apidae
Length:	0.3–2.5 cm (1/8–1 in)
Number of species:	1,000

Bumblebees live in colonies in underground nests. The queen uses nectar and pollen to make food called beebread. When her eggs hatch, the larvae feed on the beebread.

Large and hairy body is usually black, with some yellow markings

Cuckoo bee resembles a wasp

CUCKOO BEE

Family:	Anthrophoridae
Length:	0.9–1.2 cm (3/8–1/2 in)
Number of species:	4,200

This bee lays its eggs in bumblebee nests. They hatch before the bumblebees' eggs and the larvae eat up all the food stored for the bumblebee larvae. Worker bumblebees raise the cuckoo bee larvae.

Orchid bees feed on the nectar of orchid flowers

ORCHID BEE

Family:	Apidae
Length:	0.3–2.5 cm (1/8–1 in)
Number of species:	1,000

Most orchid bees live in the tropics and are brightly coloured. The males visit orchid plants to feed on their flowers. They also pollinate the flowers and collect a substance that they turn into scent to attract female bees.

Females use their jaws to cut pieces from roses, beech hedges and other plants

LEAFCUTTER BEE

Family:	Megachilidae
Length:	0.9–2 cm (3/8–3/4 in)
Number of species:	3,000

Pieces are oval or semicircular

This bee tunnels a nest into soil or rotten wood. It then builds sausage-shaped cells for its larvae, using pieces cut from leaves and flowers. Pollen and nectar are placed in each cell, and an egg is laid on top. The larvae eat the pollen and nectar when they hatch.

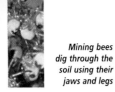

Mining bees dig through the soil using their jaws and legs

Mining bees nest in long branching tunnels that they dig in the ground, often leaving a tiny pile of fine soil around the entrance. Each bee digs its own nest, but large numbers may live close together.

The abdomen of bees, wasps and ants narrows at the top to form a "waist"

MINING BEE

Family:	Andrenidae
Length:	0.3–2 cm (1/8–3/4 in)
Number of species:	4,000

Workers gather nectar and pollen

A honey bee colony has an egg-laying queen, a few males (drones) and lots of sterile females called workers. A worker lives for only 6–8 weeks. First she cares for the eggs and larvae. Then she helps to build and clean the nest. Finally, she becomes a food gatherer.

HONEY BEE

Family:	Apidae
Length:	0.3–2.5 cm (1/8–1 in)
Number of species:	1,000

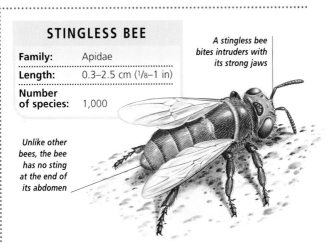

STINGLESS BEE

Family:	Apidae
Length:	0.3–2.5 cm (1/8–1 in)
Number of species:	1,000

A stingless bee bites intruders with its strong jaws

Unlike other bees, the bee has no sting at the end of its abdomen

Stingless bees live in colonies. They make their nests in holes in the ground and hollow tree trunks, sometimes even in part of a termite mound. The worker bees leave a trail of scent between a food source and their nest, so other workers can find the food.

CARPENTER BEE

Family:	Apidae
Length:	0.3–2.5 cm (1/8–1 in)
Number of species:	1,000

These large bees fly noisily from flower to flower collecting nectar

The carpenter bee gets its name because the female chews a tunnel-like nest in wood. She makes a line of separate cells inside the tunnel, and lays one egg in each cell She stays nearby to guard the nest until the larvae hatch from the eggs.

Giant hornets nest in trees or old buildings and feed on nectar and insects. They also strip bark off shrubs and lick up the sap. In summer, they fly at night and are attracted by light.

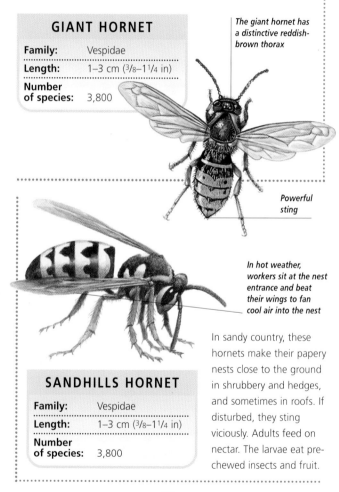

GIANT HORNET

Family:	Vespidae
Length:	1–3 cm (3/8–1 1/4 in)
Number of species:	3,800

The giant hornet has a distinctive reddish-brown thorax

Powerful sting

In hot weather, workers sit at the nest entrance and beat their wings to fan cool air into the nest

SANDHILLS HORNET

Family:	Vespidae
Length:	1–3 cm (3/8–1 1/4 in)
Number of species:	3,800

In sandy country, these hornets make their papery nests close to the ground in shrubbery and hedges, and sometimes in roofs. If disturbed, they sting viciously. Adults feed on nectar. The larvae eat pre-chewed insects and fruit.

Wasps use their stings to kill or paralyse prey, as well as in self-defence

The female spider wasp hunts spiders, and may even attack a spider in its own lair. She paralyses it with her sting and drags it back to a nest cell. She lays an egg in the cell and seals the cell with mud. When the egg hatches, the larva eats the spider. The adults feed on nectar.

BLUE-BLACK SPIDER WASP

Family:	Pompilidae
Length:	0.9–5 cm (3/8–2 in)
Number of species:	4,000

These solitary, unaggressive wasps feed on other insects and nectar. The female builds a nest using balls of damp mud or clay. She lays a single egg in each cell in the nest, adding some paralysed insects for the larva to eat when it hatches.

MUD DAUBER

Family:	Sphecidae
Length:	0.9–5 cm (3/8–2 in)
Number of species:	8,000

Many mud daubers have long, slender waists

COMMON WASP/ YELLOW JACKET

Family:	Vespidae
Length:	1–3 cm (3/8–11/4 in)
Number of species:	3,800

Common wasps feed on nectar and sweet food, such as ripe apples

These wasps are known for their sting, which they use for killing prey and self-defence. If a colony is disturbed, sentry wasps fly out and sting the intruder. The venom contains an "alarm" chemical. Other wasps detect this chemical and sting around the same site.

GALL WASP

Some galls provide food and protection for up to 30 wasp larvae

Family:	Cynipidae
Length:	0.15–0.9 cm (1/16–3/8 in)
Number of species:	1,250

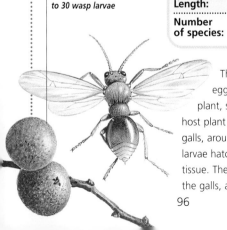

These tiny wasps lay their eggs on particular species of plant, such as oak trees. The host plant forms growths, called galls, around the eggs. When the larvae hatch, they feed on the gall tissue. They develop in safety inside the galls, and emerge as adults.

Body has a velvety covering of thick hair

Despite its name, the velvet ant is actually a wasp. It lays its eggs on the larvae of bees and other wasps. When the velvet ant larvae hatch, they eat their hosts. The females are wingless, but the males are fully winged and can fly.

Wingless female looks a bit like an ant

VELVET ANT

Family:	Mutillidae
Length:	0.6–2.5 cm (1/4–1 in)
Number of species:	5,000

Unlike other wasps, sawflies have no "waist" between the thorax and the abdomen. The female has sawlike blades on her ovipositor, which she uses to insert eggs into plants. The larvae resemble moth caterpillars.

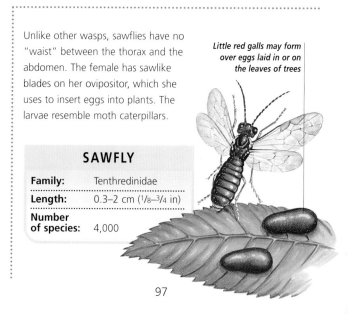

Little red galls may form over eggs laid in or on the leaves of trees

SAWFLY

Family:	Tenthredinidae
Length:	0.3–2 cm (1/8–3/4 in)
Number of species:	4,000

SNOUTED TERMITE

Family: Termitidae

Length: up to 6 cm (2½ in)

**Number
of species:** 1,650

In most termite colonies, workers look after the nest and find food, while soldiers protect them. Snouted termite soldiers immobilise attackers such as ants with a sticky, poisonous liquid that they spray from their long snouts.

Soldier

*Most soldier
and worker
termites are blind*

Termites have special microorganisms in their gut to help them digest cellulose, the tough material that forms the bulk of plants. Drywood termites perform a valuable "waste disposal" service by eating dead wood. But they can also do great damage when they feed on furniture and wooden buildings.

Worker

Soldier

*Soldier termites have
larger heads and jaws
than the workers*

DRYWOOD TERMITE

Family: Kalotermitidae

Length: up to 2.5 cm (1 in)

**Number
of Species:** 8,800

SUBTERRANEAN TERMITE

Soldier

Family:	Rhinotermitidae
Length:	0.6–0.9 cm (1/4–3/8 in)
Number of Species:	200

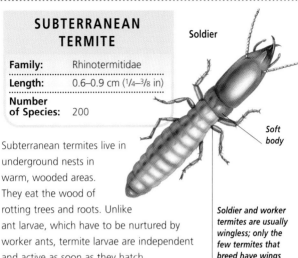

Subterranean termites live in underground nests in warm, wooded areas. They eat the wood of rotting trees and roots. Unlike ant larvae, which have to be nurtured by worker ants, termite larvae are independent and active as soon as they hatch.

Soft body

Soldier and worker termites are usually wingless; only the few termites that breed have wings

CARPENTER ANT

Family:	Formicidae
Length:	0.15–2.5 cm (1/16–1 in)
Number of species:	8,800

Colonies of carpenter ants make their nests in wooden buildings and rotting trees. Like many ants, they lay scent trails as they scurry around in search of food. Other ants sense the trails with their antennae and follow them between the nest and the food.

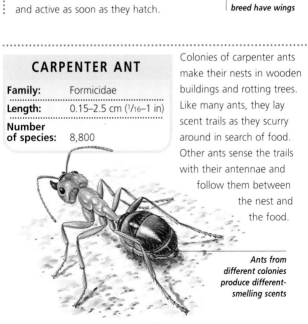

Ants from different colonies produce different-smelling scents

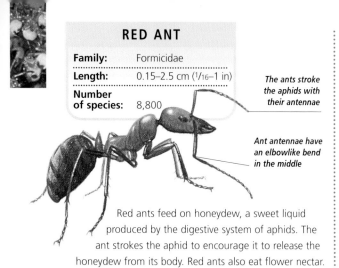

RED ANT

Family:	Formicidae
Length:	0.15–2.5 cm (¹⁄₁₆–1 in)
Number of species:	8,800

The ants stroke the aphids with their antennae

Ant antennae have an elbowlike bend in the middle

Red ants feed on honeydew, a sweet liquid produced by the digestive system of aphids. The ant strokes the aphid to encourage it to release the honeydew from its body. Red ants also eat flower nectar.

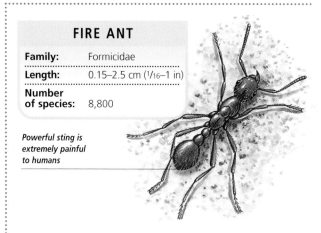

FIRE ANT

Family:	Formicidae
Length:	0.15–2.5 cm (¹⁄₁₆–1 in)
Number of species:	8,800

Powerful sting is extremely painful to humans

The aggressive fire ant feeds on other insects, which it stings to death. It bites to secure itself and then inserts its stinging apparatus into the wound and injects venom. It also eats seeds, fruit and flowers. It makes its nest in the ground or under logs and stones.

HARVESTER ANT

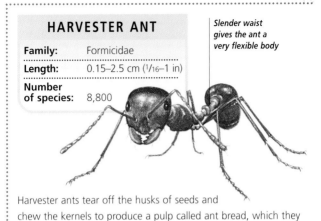

Family: Formicidae

Length: 0.15–2.5 cm ($^{1}/_{16}$–1 in)

Number of species: 8,800

Slender waist gives the ant a very flexible body

Harvester ants tear off the husks of seeds and chew the kernels to produce a pulp called ant bread, which they then swallow. In times of plenty, they collect more seeds than they need and store the excess in special granary chambers in the nest.

Strong, scissorlike jaws

The ant will hold the leaf piece above its head as it carries it back to the nest

LEAFCUTTER ANT

Family: Formicidae

Length: 0.15–2.5 cm ($^{1}/_{16}$–1 in)

Number of species: 8,800

Leafcutter ants cut pieces from leaves and carry them back to their underground nest. They chew up the leaves and mix them with their droppings to make a special compost. The ants feed on the fungus that grows on these compost "gardens".

Spiders and scorpions

Spiders are famed for their silk-spinning skills and poisonous bites. Like scorpions, ticks and mites, they are not insects but arachnids.

WOLF SPIDER

Family:	Lycosidae
Length:	0.3–4 cm ($^{1}/_{8}$–1$^{1}/_{2}$ in)
Number of species:	2,500

Large eyes help to spot prey

The fast-moving wolf spider creeps up on its prey and then seizes it after a final burst of speed. The wolf spider has better vision than most spiders. Even so, its eyes respond mainly to movement, so insects that remain still are more likely to escape.

A jumping spider secures itself to a surface with a silken safety line and pushes off with its back four legs to leap on to its prey. Some jumping spiders can leap more than 40 times their own length.

JUMPING SPIDER

Family:	Salticidae
Length:	0.3–1.5 cm ($^{1}/_{8}$–$^{5}/_{8}$ in)
Number of species:	4,000

BLACK WIDOW SPIDER

Family:	Theridiidae
Length:	up to 1.2 cm ($\frac{1}{2}$ in)
Number of species:	2,500

The female black widow's venomous bite is 15 times more powerful than rattlesnake venom and is capable of killing a person. Fortunately, the black widow is a shy creature and will usually attack only if disturbed. Male black widows do not bite. The female is thought to eat the male after mating.

Female's back legs have comblike bristles, which she uses to throw silk strands over prey

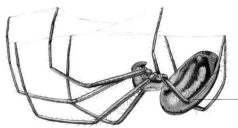

Spider may release a special scent that attracts moths

ORCHARD SPIDER

Family:	Araeneidae
Length:	0.15–3 cm ($\frac{1}{16}$–1$\frac{1}{4}$ in)
Number of species:	2,500

Unlike other members of the orb-weaver family, which weave intricate webs, the orchard spider does not use silk to catch its prey. It simply sits in full view on the branch of a tree and grabs any moth that comes within reach of its spiny front legs.

RED-KNEED TARANTULA

Family:	Theraphosidae
Length:	up to 9 cm (3½ in)
Number of species:	300

With its hind legs, a tarantula can flick prickly hairs off its abdomen at attackers

The red-kneed tarantula preys on lizards, mice and even small birds. Tarantulas are among the largest of all spiders, with legs spanning more than 20 cm (8 in). Most hide during the day, often in burrows, and hunt prey at night, which they kill with venom. The venom is not usually fatal to humans.

Fangs at the tips of the jaws inject venom

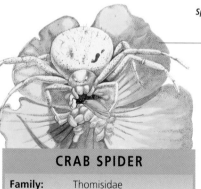

Spider's yellow colouring blends with the bright flower petals

CRAB SPIDER

Family:	Thomisidae
Length:	0.15–0.9 cm (¹⁄₁₆–³⁄₈ in)
Number of species:	3,000

These small, crablike spiders have broad, flat bodies and scuttle sideways when they move. Instead of a web, they use stealth and strong venom to catch prey. Some are dark brown or black, but those that hunt on flowers have bright colours for camouflage.

GREEN LYNX SPIDER

Family:	Oxyopidae
Length:	0.3–1.5 cm ($^1/_8$–$^5/_8$ in)
Number of species:	500

Long legs for jumping between leaves

Instead of building a web to catch prey, lynx spiders chase insects and spiders over plants, jumping from leaf to leaf. Camouflaged by their colouring, they may also sit and wait for prey. These "cannibals" will even eat members of their own species.

SPITTING SPIDER

Family:	Scytodidae
Length:	0.9 cm ($^3/_8$ in)
Number of species:	200

This spider spits two zigzagging lines of gluey liquid over its prey from glands near its mouth. The glue pins down the prey, and the spider then kills it with a poisonous bite.

GOLDEN-SILK SPIDER

Family:	Araeneidae
Length:	0.15–3 cm ($^1/_{16}$–$1^1/_4$ in)
Number of species:	2,500

The male golden-silk spider is about one-eighth of the size of the female and weighs 100 times less. When mating, his small size allows him to approach her without being mistaken for a large attacker.

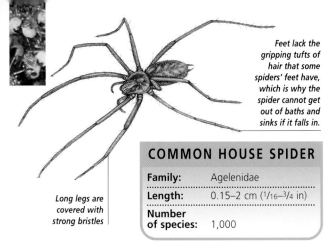

Feet lack the gripping tufts of hair that some spiders' feet have, which is why the spider cannot get out of baths and sinks if it falls in.

COMMON HOUSE SPIDER

Family:	Agelenidae
Length:	0.15–2 cm (1/16–3/4 in)
Number of species:	1,000

Long legs are covered with strong bristles

The house spider may live for several years in a quiet corner of a house, garage or shed. It builds a large, flat web and waits for prey such as earwigs, flies and other household pests to get tangled-up in the sticky web strands. The spider then removes and eats the prey.

PURSE-WEB SPIDER

Family:	Atypidae
Length:	0.9–3 cm (3/8–1 1/4 in)
Number of species:	1

Purse-web is less hairy than many spiders

Sharp fangs stab into prey

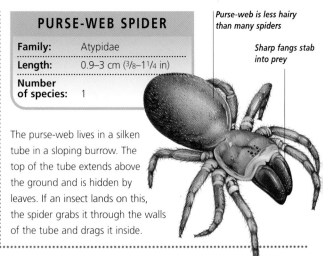

The purse-web lives in a silken tube in a sloping burrow. The top of the tube extends above the ground and is hidden by leaves. If an insect lands on this, the spider grabs it through the walls of the tube and drags it inside.

106

WATER SPIDER

Family:	Agelenidae
Length:	0.15–2 cm (^{1}/16–^{3}/4 in)
Number of species:	1,000

Spider attaches the sac to water plants and fills it with air from the surface

This spider spends its life underwater, living in a bell-shaped sac of silk. It pounces on passing prey and drags it into the bell to devour it.

NURSERY-WEB SPIDER

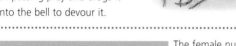

Family:	Pisauridae
Length:	0.6–2.5 cm (^{1}/4–1 in)
Number of species:	400

Egg-sac is speared by the fangs and held by the pedipalps

The female nursery-web spider carries her egg-sac around until the eggs are ready to hatch. She spins a protective web over them and stands guard by the "nursery" of newly hatched spiderlings.

Most spiders have eight eyes, but the cell spider has only six. By day, it hides in a silken cell under a stone – usually one that will be warmed by the sun. It emerges at night to hunt for woodlice, which it impales on its sharp fangs.

CELL SPIDER

Family:	Dysderidae
Length:	2 cm (^{3}/4 in)
Number of species:	1

Enormous fangs pierce the tough outer skeleton of woodlice

107

SCORPION

Family:	Buthidae
Length:	5–7 cm (2–2 3/4 in)
Number of species:	700

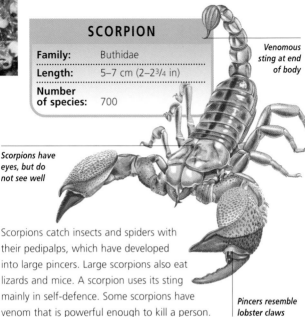

Venomous sting at end of body

Scorpions have eyes, but do not see well

Scorpions catch insects and spiders with their pedipalps, which have developed into large pincers. Large scorpions also eat lizards and mice. A scorpion uses its sting mainly in self-defence. Some scorpions have venom that is powerful enough to kill a person.

Pincers resemble lobster claws

WIND SCORPION

Family:	Eremobatidae
Length:	1.5–4.5 cm (5/8–1 3/4 in)
Number of species:	900

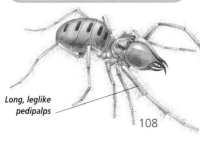

Long, leglike pedipalps

The fast-running wind scorpion is related to true scorpions. It lives in desert areas and hunts insects and even small lizards by night. It catches prey with its pedipalps and crushes it to death with its jaws. Only three pairs of legs are used for walking – the front pair are used as feelers.

Instead of an arching sting, the whip scorpion has a long, thin, whiplike tail

The whip scorpion is not a true scorpion and has no sting. It has eight legs, but the long front pair are used as feelers. If attacked, it sprays a vinegary liquid from glands near the base of its tail, which is why it is also known as the vinegaroon.

WHIP SCORPION

Family:	Thelyphonidae
Length:	14.5 cm (5³/4 in)
Number of species:	100

Pedipalps contain venom glands

Pseudoscorpions are tiny, stingless relatives of the scorpion. They live in the soil but cling to beetles, flies or harvestmen to hitch a ride from place to place. They spin cocoons in which to spend the winter, using silk glands in their mouthparts.

Pseudoscorpion darts backwards when attacked from the front

PSEUDOSCORPION

Family:	Chernetidae
Length:	up to 0.6 cm (1/4 in)
Number of species:	1,000

VELVET MITE

Family:	Trombiculidae
Length:	up to 0.5 cm ($^3/_{16}$ in)
Number of species:	200

Velvet mite's body has a coat of thick, soft hairs

Velvet mites are related to spiders. Adults feed mostly on insect eggs and lay their eggs on the ground. Although the adults are free-living, the larvae are parasitic and feed on the body fluids of spiders.

Long body hairs are touch-sensitive

HOUSE DUST MITE

Family:	Pyroglyphidae
Length:	up to 0.5 mm ($^2/_{100}$ in)
Number of species:	20

Mites usually have flat or rounded bodies and gripping legs. The house dust mite feeds on scales of skin found in house dust. Its droppings contain substances that cause an allergic reaction or asthma (difficulty in breathing) in some people.

HARVESTMAN

Family:	Phalangiidae
Length:	0.3–2 cm ($^{1}/_{8}$–$^{3}/_{4}$ in)
Number of species:	3,400

All its legs are very long, but the second pair are the longest

This spiderlike arachnid has only two eyes on a turretlike projection in the middle of its body. The harvestman has no venom, but can protect itself by giving off a nasty smell from its scent glands. Females lay their eggs in the ground, where they stay throughout the winter until they hatch the next spring.

The harvestman detects and traps insect prey with its legs

Tick clings on to its moving host with its strong mouthparts

TICK

Family:	Ixodidae
Length:	0.15–0.3 cm ($^{1}/_{16}$–$^{1}/_{8}$ in)
Number of species:	650

Ticks are parasitic, living off reptiles, mammals, and birds. They wait on plants and climb on to an animal as it brushes past. The tick pierces the host animal's skin with its serrated jaws and then feeds on its blood.

Glossary

abdomen The rear section of an insect's body, behind the head and thorax.

algae Simple plantlike living things.

anal claspers Gripping, suckerlike projections at the end of the body of caterpillars and male dragonflies.

antennae (*singular* antenna) A pair of sensitive structures on an insect's head. They help the insect to sense things about its surroundings by smell, taste and touch.

arachnid An arthropod with eight legs. Spiders, scorpions, ticks and mites are arachnids.

arthropod An invertebrate animal with an exoskeleton.

camouflage The means by which an animal's colour, patterning or shape help it to blend in with its surroundings.

cannibals Animals that eat members of their own species.

carnivores Meat-eating animals.

carrion The flesh of dead animals.

caterpillar The larva of a moth or butterfly.

cell A six-sided space in the nest of a bee or wasp, often used to store food or eggs.

cephalothorax Part of an arachnid's body. It is the head and thorax fused together.

chamber Section of a nest of insects such as ants and termites. There are separate chambers for rearing young, storing food, and so on.

cocoon A silken case that protects the pupae of insects such as moths.

colony A group of insects living together in a nest. Ants, termites and some wasps and bees live in colonies.

compound eyes Eyes that are made up of hundreds of different parts, each with a tiny lens on the surface.

courtship Animal behaviour that leads to the selection of a mate and to mating.

drone A male bee who mates with the queen and does not join in the work of the colony.

egg-sac A silken bag or pouch, which a female spider spins around her eggs to protect them.

egg tooth A temporary tooth that a baby spider uses to pierce the shell of its egg.

exoskeleton The tough outer casing of an arthropod's body, which protects the muscles and organs inside.

false-eye spots Blobs of colour on an insect's body or wings. Predators mistake these spots for the eyes of a larger animal and stay away.

fangs Pointed mouthparts, often hollow for injecting venom into prey.

fossil The preserved remains of a dead animal or plant. Fossils are found in rocks and amber (solidified tree sap).

fungi Simple living things that are not green plants and not animals. Mushrooms and toadstools are types of fungi.

gall A growth that forms on a plant, around eggs laid by certain types of wasps.

gland A part of the body that produces special substances, such as enzymes and poisons, which pass either outside of the body or into the blood. A scorpion's venom gland, for example, makes poison which the scorpion injects into victims with its sting.

grub A term used to describe many insect larvae, especially beetle, wasp and bee larvae.

halteres A pair of small, knobbed structures, one on each side of a fly's body. They help a fly to control its flight.

hibernate A sleeplike state that helps some animals to survive the winter.

host An animal on or in which a parasite lives and feeds.

insect An arthropod with six legs and a body arranged into three distinct parts – head, thorax and abdomen.

invertebrate An animal without a backbone. Insects, arachnids, worms, snails and slugs are all invertebrates.

larvae (*singular* larva) Young insects that look very different from their adult forms. They moult several times and become pupae, before emerging as adults.

mating The coming together of male and female animals to produce young.

metamorphosis The change of a young insect through several growth stages into its adult form.

microorganisms Tiny lifeforms that cannot be seen without a microscope. They include bacteria and some types of algae and fungi.

migration The movement of animals in search of food or warmer weather.

mimicry The use of colours and patterns to copy another animal's appearance.

moulting Shedding an old skin in its entirety, to reveal a new skin underneath.

nectar A sugary liquid produced by plants that attracts pollinating insects.

nymph The larva of insects such as dragonflies and grasshoppers. Nymphs develop into adults without first becoming pupae.

ovipositor The egg-laying tube of most female insects.

paralyse To affect an animal's nervous system so that it cannot move, but is still alive.

parasites Creatures, such as fleas or ticks, that live and feed on or inside other living creatures.

pedipalps Projecting sense organs in arachnids. Some arachnids also use pedipalps to grasp objects such as prey.

pesticides Chemicals used by farmers to kill insect pests.

pheromone A chemical that some animals produce to attract a mate.

pollen Tiny grains made by the male parts of a flower. Pollen must reach the female parts of a flower for seeds to form. Bees, wasps, flies and other insects help this process by carrying pollen between flowers as they feed.

predator An animal that hunts other animals for food.

prey The victim of a predator.

proboscis The tubelike mouthparts of moths, butterflies and some flies.

prolegs Muscular stumps on a caterpillar's body that help it to hold on to twigs and leaves.

pupa (*plural* pupae) The stage at which a larva changes into an adult.

queen An egg-laying female in a colony of ants, bees, wasps or termites.

saliva A colourless liquid made by glands in the mouth that helps to digest food.

sap A nutrient-rich liquid found in plants.

sensory hairs Tiny hairs attached to nerves that enable insects and arachnids to detect things by touch.

silk Threads of protein made by spiders and some insects.

simple eyes Eyes with only one lens. Spiders and some insects have simple eyes.

species A particular type of animal or plant. Members of the same species can mate and produce young that are able to continue to breed.

spinnerets Tubes at the end of a spider's abdomen, through which the spider squeezes silk to spin a web.

spiracles Tiny breathing holes on an insect's abdomen.

sterile Adult animals that are unable to breed.

sting The sharp body part of an insect or scorpion, used to inject venom into attackers or prey.

territory An area an animal defends against intruders.

thorax The middle section of an insect's body.

true bugs A group of insects with needlelike mouthparts. "Bug" is used generally to refer to any insect or arachnid.

tymbals Drumlike structures on the legs of some insects used to produce mating calls.

venom A poisonous liquid used by an animal to kill or paralyse prey.

vertebrate An animal with a backbone and internal skeleton, such as a mammal, bird, amphibian or reptile.

web A network of silken threads woven by a spider and used to trap prey.

wing cases The hard coverings of a beetle's hind wings. They are formed from the beetle's fore wings, which are no longer used for flight.

workers The insects in a social colony that build the nest, find food and care for the young. There are worker bees, ants and termites.

Index

117

International museums

Here are just a few museums with good collections of bugs. Exhibits may change as collections are added to, and bug exhibitions may tour different museums.

AUSTRALIA
Australia Museum, Sydney, New South Wales
Queensland Museum, Brisbane, Queensland

CANADA
Newfoundland Insectarium, Deer Lake, Newfoundland
Redpath Museum, Quebec
Royal Ontario Museum, Toronto, Ontario

UNITED KINGDOM
Booth Museum of Natural History, Brighton, England
Castle Museum, Norwich, England
Manchester Museum, University of Manchester, England
National Museum of Wales, Cardiff, Wales
Natural History Museum London, England
Oxford University Museum of Natural History, Oxford, England
Royal Scottish Museum, Edinburgh, Scotland

UNITED STATES OF AMERICA
American Museum of Natural History, New York
Carnegie Museum of Natural History, Pittsburgh, Pennsylvania
Minibeast Zooseum and Educational Centre, Lancing, Michigan
Natural History Museum of Los Angeles County, Los Angeles, California
Peabody Museum of Natural History, New Haven, Connecticut
National Museum of Natural History, Washington, DC
Utah Museum of Natural History, Salt Lake City, Utah

Web sites

Web sites are constantly being expanded or added to. Check out:

http://members.aol.com/YESbugs/bugclub.html
Home page of the USA's Young Entomologists Society

http://info.ex.ac.uk/bugclub/main.html
Home page of the Bug Club, a branch of the UK's Amateur Entomologists Society

http://www.nhusd.k12.ca.us/cabell/~kidlinks/scilink.html
Links to science sites, with many on bugs

www.insect-world.com/
Fairly advanced site full of in-depth information on insects and arachnids

Acknowledgements

The author would like to thank Oliver Cheeseman of CABI Bioscience, Ascot, England, for help and advice in the writing of this book.

ARTISTS
Robin Boutell, Richard Coombes, Joanne Cowne, Sandra Doyle, Bridget James, Anne Jennings, Elizabeth Kay, Steve Kirk, Adrian Lascom, Alan Male, Colin Newman, Obin, Steve Roberts, Bernard Robinson, Eric Robson, Roger Stewart, Michael Woods, Colin Woolf

PHOTOGRAPHS
9 Sinclair Stammers/Science Photo Library; 11 Pascal Goetgheluck/Ardea; 14 Ken Preston—Mafham/Premaphotos Wildlife; 14/15 Stephen Dalton/Oxford Scientific Films; 19 Claude Nuridsany & Marie Perennon/Science Photo Library; 22 Irvine Cushing/Oxford Scientific Films; 23 Adrian Warren/Ardea; 34 Harold Taylor/Oxford Scientific Films; 35 Ken Preston-Mafham/Premaphotos Wildlife; 37, 39 Claude Nuridsany & Marie Perennon/Science Photo Library; 47 KG. Preston-Mafham/Premaphotos Wildlife